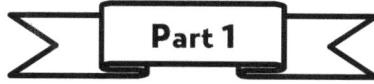

The **Feast** of

Wisdom

101 Biblical Answers To Common Questions Many Believers Ask

COLETTE A. GUTHRIE

DAYELight

PUBLISHERS

ISBN: 978-1-966723-17-2 (paperback)

ACKNOWLEDGMENTS

To Coach Crystal Daye, thank you for sparking the idea for this book.

To the Kencot Seventh-day Adventist Church's Personal Ministries team, thanks for giving me the opportunity to write Bible lessons for Revelation seminars.

To all my friends who have asked me Bible questions, thank you.

TABLE OF CONTENTS

Rejoice···

INTRODUCTION

Today, we live in a world where people with questions often default to one trusted source when seeking answers: they turn to the internet. Can you relate?

If you are old enough, you may have memories of visits to a public library. I remember visiting the library in my rural community while in primary school. These trips took place after school on weekday afternoons, on scheduled "library days."

I often reached the library before the doors opened at 3 pm and had to wait in the warm afternoon sun. The goal was to find and borrow the popular books. I read much fiction in my childhood, primarily mystery novels. Sometimes I peeked at the back of the book so that I wouldn't have to wait for days to find out how the story ended.

Online, the answers to questions may vary, depending on the search parameters that are used. Over time, people from all walks of life have found answers to their questions of faith in the Bible, the world's biggest bestseller. The Bible is the only constant, unchanging guide we have to help us navigate the uncertain times in which we live. In the Bible, the reader can find the truth.

My primary goal for this book is to equip each Bible student to answer the key questions of faith by carefully studying several Bible verses. Join me on this culinary adventure through the book of Ecclesiastes as we explore lessons from the world of food and drink.

ABOUT THE BIBLE

- The Bible is a collection of 66 books in one binding.

- About 40 different authors wrote the Bible over a period of 1500 years.

- Each Bible writer wrote in his native language—Hebrew, Aramaic, or Greek.

- These writers came from various backgrounds, different levels of education, and different cultures.

- Scripture is not the thoughts and ideas of these individual men: "*for prophecy never came by the will of man, but holy men of God spoke as they were moved by the Holy Spirit.*" (2 Peter 1:21 – NKJV).

BIBLE STUDY PRINCIPLES

"The word of God is plain to all who study it with a prayerful heart."

—Ellen G. White

It is important to follow the following principles when reading and studying the Bible:

1. **Always ask** for the guidance of the Holy Spirit before studying the Bible because the Bible is the inspired Word of God.

2. **Approach** Bible study with an attitude of humility and an open mind, seeking to learn, never with preconceived ideas nor with pride of opinion.

3. **Ask** questions as you read and study, and diligently seek the answers.

4. **Apply** all Scripture passages or verses on a topic to clarify a subject.

5. **Amplify** the meaning of words through the use of tools such as a Strong's concordance, Hebrew and Greek dictionaries, Bible commentaries, and computer programs. All these will greatly enhance our studies.

6. **Ascertain** the context of a passage. A passage is a group of verses. We must be careful not to take one or more verses out of their "context" and use them to teach something unrelated to the subject matter of the passage.

7. **Allow** the Bible to interpret itself rather than depending on speculation and guesswork.

8. **Acquaint** yourself with Jesus—a personal, intimate relationship with Him is the main aim of Bible study.

9. *Apparent* **discrepancies** may often be explained by a careful study of the entire Bible, comparing verse with verse so that all the available evidence is obtained rather than looking at only one or two verses and possibly drawing the wrong conclusions.

10. **Allow** yourself enough time to study the Bible for yourself. A superficial reading of the Bible will only result in a superficial understanding of the Bible.

ABOUT THE BOOK OF ECCLESIASTES

"The words of the Preacher, the son of David, king in Jerusalem. Vanity of vanities, saith the Preacher, vanity of vanities; all is vanity." (Ecclesiastes 1:1-2 - KJV).

The Hebrew title of the book, *Qoheleth*, is a rare term found only in Ecclesiastes (see Ecclesiastes 1:1, 2, 12; 7:27 and 12:8-10). It comes from the word *qahal*, meaning "to convoke an assembly, to assemble." Thus, it means "One who addresses an assembly," "A preacher."[1]

WHO WROTE THE BOOK OF ECCLESIASTES?

Ecclesiastes records the words of Qohelet—the Preacher (traditionally taken to be Solomon—Ecclesiastes 1:1,12—the wisest, richest, most influential king in Israel's history). The book's author presents Qohelet's teachings and also offers his own conclusions in Ecclesiastes 12:9-14.[2]

KEY THEMES

The key word in Ecclesiastes is *vanity*, "the futile emptiness of trying to be happy apart from God." The preacher looks at life "under the sun" (see Ecclesiastes 1:9) and, from the human perspective, declares it all to be empty. Power, popularity, prestige, pleasure–nothing can fill the God-shaped void in man's life but God Himself!

---

[1] Thomas Nelson KJV Reference Bible, Introduction to Ecclesiastes

[2] "BibleProject Guides - Guide to the Book of Ecclesiastes", https://bibleproject.com/guides/book-of-ecclesiastes/

Once seen from God's perspective, life takes on meaning and purpose, causing Solomon to exclaim. *"Eat ... drink ... rejoice ... do good ... live joyfully ... fear God ... keep His commandments!"* Scepticism and despair melt away when life is viewed as a daily gift from God.[3]

---

[3] Thomas Nelson KJV Reference Bible, Introduction to Ecclesiastes

FEAR GOD ...

" ... fear thou God." (Ecclesiastes 5:7 - KJV).

Recipe For Success

"And further, by these, my son, be admonished: of making many books there is no end; and much study is a weariness of the flesh." (Ecclesiastes 12:12 - KJV).

I developed a love for reading and books at an early age. After high school, I started collecting cookbooks and recipes of all types.

DID YOU KNOW?

- The oldest known written recipes, which were carved in clay tablets in Mesopotamia from 1700 BC, were prepared for religious rites.

- Cookbooks are primarily collections of culinary recipes— written instructions often based on earlier oral communication. Today they are handwritten, printed, or digitised in various forms on the internet.

- Printed cookbooks were first published in Europe in the fifteenth century and later spread globally.

- Most cookbooks include recipes for a variety of culinary products, but there are also special books on one particular food, on a single dish, and on special diets such as vegetarian, vegan, kosher, and halal.

- Cookbooks are important sources that trace the development of culinary traditions. Apart from the practical instructions, cookbooks contain historical statements and references to social status, health, local produce, manners and customs, religion, taste, and aesthetics.[4]

DIGGING DEEPER

The world's biggest bestseller—the Bible—was written in a way that enables it to speak to people in every period of history, language, and culture.

In this study, we will examine the origin and purpose of the Word of God.

   1. *Where did we get the Scriptures from?*

"for prophecy never came by the will of man, but holy men of God spoke as they were moved by the Holy Spirit." (2 Peter 1:21 - NKJV).

The Bible is not a word-for-word dictation from God, but rather God speaking through the human mind, with each writer expressing the thoughts they received in their own way.

In Ecclesiastes 12:11, Solomon said that his collections of wise sayings were given by one Shepherd. God is the Shepherd of His people, the One who nourishes, guides, and protects (see Psalm 23:1 and Isaiah 40:11). God is the ultimate source of all wisdom. We have Scripture to reveal God, His plan, and His purpose for our lives.[5]

---

[4] "History of Cookbooks",
https://oxfordre.com/foodstudies/display/10.1093/acrefore/9780197762530.001.0001/acrefore-9780197762530-e-16
[5] https://bsop.edu.ph/lasting-lessons-from-life-ecclesiastes-111-1214/#:~

2. Why is it necessary to study the Scriptures?

"Study to shew thyself approved unto God, a workman that needeth not to be ashamed, rightly dividing the word of truth." (2 Timothy 2:15 - KJV)

God wants us to base our faith on something solid—the sure word of prophecy. He also wants us to reason with Him (see Isaiah 1:18) and to come to a correct understanding of the Scriptures for ourselves.

3. What benefit can be obtained from studying the Scriptures?

"And that from a child thou hast known the holy Scriptures, which are able to make thee wise unto salvation through faith which is in Christ Jesus." (2 Timothy 3:15 - KJV)

We are saved by grace through faith in Jesus Christ (see Ephesians 2:8). Faith grows when the Scriptures are proclaimed and the Word of God is heard (see Romans 10:17). The proclamation of the gospel opens the door of salvation for all who accept the gospel message.

4. What other benefits do studying the Scriptures provide?

"All scripture is given by inspiration of God, and is profitable for doctrine, for reproof, for correction, for instruction in righteousness: That the man of God may be perfect, throughly furnished unto all good works." (2 Timothy 3:16-17 - KJV).

The Scriptures are like a complete toolkit, with a variety of verses for multiple functions, including teaching, training, guiding believers, and education in principles of right living. As a result of following the Bible's principles, the man, woman, or child of God *"may be complete, trained and made ready for every good work"* in the kingdom of God. The Word of God is the greatest lesson book that we could ever learn from.

5. *What reason did Peter give for studying the Scriptures?*

"But in your hearts revere Christ as Lord. Always be prepared to give an answer to everyone who asks you to give the reason for the hope that you have. But do this with gentleness and respect." (1 Peter 3:15 – NIV)

One reason a believer has to study the Scriptures is to answer questions people may ask about his or her faith in Jesus. This should always be done with childlike humility.

6. *What is the right way to study the Bible?*

"For precept must be upon precept, precept upon precept; line upon line, line upon line; here a little, and there a little." (Isaiah 28:10 - KJV).

When doing Bible studies, especially topical Bible studies, each topic should be studied holistically, taking a verse-by-verse approach.

7. *What pitfalls should be avoided when studying the Scriptures?*

"Timothy, keep safe what has been entrusted to your care. Avoid the profane talk and foolish arguments of what some people wrongly call "Knowledge." For some have claimed to possess it, and as a result they have lost the way of faith." (1 Timothy 6:20-21 - GNT).

The Scriptures should not be studied in order to have a debate or win an argument. Foolish arguments, especially about things that are falsely called knowledge, should be avoided. In seeking to win an argument, many have argued their way out of the faith (see Titus 3:9).

THE LESSON

In Ecclesiastes 12:12 the author counsels his son: *"... of making many books there is no end; and much study is a weariness of the flesh." (KJV).*

Don't misunderstand what the author is saying. He is not condemning studying, learning, or reading. Rather, he is saying that endless learning only bogs us down in theory. Knowledge of the Scriptures without the application of its principles is useless. Application of the Word of God to our daily lives is the key to true success (see Joshua 1:8).

THE TAKEAWAY

It is more important to live what we learn than to learn everything. This is the way to fix the wise sayings of God firmly in our minds (see Ecclesiastes 12:11).

A Seat At The Table

"Where the word of a king is, there is power; And who may say to him, "What are you doing?""" (Ecclesiastes 8:4 - NKJV)

DID YOU KNOW?

- Some of the career paths you could choose within the culinary arts include cook or chef, restaurant owner or manager, recipe developer, cookbook author, food writer or blogger, food photographer, food manufacturer, chef consultant, and food stylist.[6]

CAREER PATHS

I recently attended a two-day training session where I was asked, *"If you had the opportunity to choose a different career path, what would you choose?"* I told my learning partner that before choosing a career in the field of accountancy, I had considered becoming a nutritionist.

One of the courses in my accountancy programme at university was politics. The most memorable topic for me was "types of electoral systems."

I learnt that there were three main types of electoral systems used globally to determine the outcome of an election: plurality, majority, and proportional representation. With proportional representation, the percentage of total votes that a political party

---

[6] "What Are The Culinary Arts?", https://www.escoffier.edu/blog/culinary-arts/what-are-the-culinary-arts/

receives is translated into the number of seats that party will have.[7] This system is used by the United States of America.

Electoral systems demonstrate who really holds the reins of power, whether it is the population as a whole (in a pure democracy) or the individual citizens (in a republic type of government).[8]

In this study, we will discover some interesting things about the government of God and how it really functions.

1. What is God really like?

"Then God said, "Let Us make man in Our image, according to Our likeness ..." (Genesis 1:26 - NKJV).

Throughout Genesis 1, *God* is translated from the Old Testament Hebrew word *Elohim*, which means "gods" (plural). The concept of God being more than one person is seen throughout the Bible, beginning with the creation accounts in Genesis 1 and 2. The term used for God is "the Godhead." In the New Testament, we find evidence that there are three members of the Godhead.

2. Who are the members of the Godhead?

"But the Helper, the Holy Spirit, whom the Father will send in My name, He will teach you all things, and bring to your remembrance all things that I said to you." (John 14:26 - NKJV).

---

[7] "Different Types of Electoral Systems", https://byjus.com/ias-questions/what-are-the-different-types-of-electoral-systems/

[8] "Republic vs. Democracy: What Is the Difference?" https://www.thoughtco.com/republic-vs-democracy-4169936

The members of the Godhead are the **Holy Spirit**, the **Father,** and **Jesus**. The three members of the Godhead have taken specific "roles" to help us, human beings, though unable to see God, to understand God and to relate to the activities of God.

We will explore some of the specific roles of the members of the Godhead in studies 3-5.

3. *How are the members of the Godhead ranked?*

"Go therefore, and make disciples of all the nations, baptizing them in the name of the Father, and of the Son, and of the Holy Spirit." (Matthew 28:19 - NKJV).

We speak of the members of the Godhead as the "first," "second," and "third" members as a way of distinguishing them from one another, not to assign them positions of rank as they are all equal.

4. *How are the members of the Godhead one?*

Even though the three members of the Godhead have taken different roles, they are a unit of three persons. From our human standpoint, it helps if we think of them as one family. Note the words of Jesus:

"Philip said to Him, "Lord, show us the Father, and it is sufficient for us." Jesus said to him, "Have I been with you so long, and yet you have not known Me, Philip? He who has seen Me has seen the Father; so how can you say, 'Show us the Father'?" (John 14:8-9 - NKJV)

Jesus said, "if you have seen Me, you have seen the Father." This is the same as saying, "if you have seen Jesus, you have seen God." Further along in the conversation, Jesus said:

23

"If you love Me, keep My commandments. And I will pray the Father, and He will give you another Helper, that He may abide with you forever." (John 14:15-16 - NKJV).

Jesus said "another Helper"–the Greek word for *another* is "allos" which means "another of the same kind." In other words, Jesus said, *"I am just like the Father, and the Spirit is just like Me!"* All three members of the Godhead are fully, equally, and eternally God.

Wherever you see the title "Father" or "Son" or "Holy Spirit," you can replace it with the word or title of "God."

5. *What is the message and mission of the Godhead?*

"For God so loved the world, that he gave his only begotten Son, that whosoever believeth in him should not perish, but have everlasting life. For God sent not his Son into the world to condemn the world; but that the world through him might be saved." (John 3:16-17 - KJV).

The message of the Godhead is love. The mission is salvation.

6. *What does the oneness of the Godhead mean for us?*

"The grace of the Lord Jesus Christ, and the love of God, and the communion of the Holy Ghost, be with you all. Amen." (2 Corinthians 13:14 - KJV).

The oneness of the Godhead means they all love us in the same way and are all working together for our salvation (see Matthew 28:19). This is the Father's plan, carried out by the Son, impressed on our hearts by the Spirit, and witnessed by the angels (see 2 Timothy 3:16). This is a good reason for us to praise God!

7. *According to Romans 2:7, what is one attribute of the Godhead that we are invited to share?*

"To them who by patient continuance in well doing seek for glory and honour and immortality, eternal life." (Romans 2:7 - KJV).

God alone is immortal (see 1 Timothy 6:16-17). Those who have faith in Jesus Christ will be rewarded with immortality (see 1 Timothy 1:16).

THE LESSON

According to Gill's commentary on Ecclesiastes 8:4, this verse is more fitting to God, the great King, than to an earthly king. The power of earthly kings makes it unwise to break their commandments. God's word of command also comes with power, and His people readily and cheerfully obey Him in response to His love (see 1 John 4:19 and John 14:15).

Unlike earthly governments, the members of the Godhead want to share their power, rights, and privileges with us. They also want us to live with them in their eternal home. Access to a seat at the table, to partake in the great supper, and to enjoy this privileged status is by invitation only (see Luke 14:15-21).

THE TAKEAWAY

Those who open the door of their hearts to allow Jesus and the Holy Spirit to come in and share a proverbial meal with them (see Revelation 3:20), feasting on the Bread of Life and drinking the Water of Life, will overcome the world, the flesh, and the Devil. They will be given a seat on the throne of God the Father (see Revelation 3:21).

Master Chef

"He has made everything beautiful in its time. ... He has put eternity in their hearts, except that no one can find out the work that God does from beginning to end." (Ecclesiastes 3:11 - NKJV).

DID YOU KNOW?

- "Chef" (French for "Chief") is traditionally a title that denotes the head of the kitchen and is generally considered a highly-skilled culinary expert.

- The chef usually creates the menu and recipes and oversees the rest of the staff.

- The cooks, on the other hand, do the prep work and much of the cooking to the chef's specifications.[9]

In my native Guyanese tradition, someone who does everything from the highest level to the lowest level is described as a *"Chief Cook and Bottlewasher."* According to Wiktionary.com, this is a humorous and informal title with unknown etymology. That person simply does it all. Writingexplained.org says the term refers to *"someone who is in power in an organisation and oversees virtually every aspect of the organisation."*

This study takes a look at the great Master Chef, God, the Father.

---

[9] "What Are The Culinary Arts?", https://www.escoffier.edu/blog/culinary-arts/what-are-the-culinary-arts/

1. Who is considered to be the first member of the Godhead?

"Yet for us there is one God, the Father, of whom are all things, and we for Him; and one Lord Jesus Christ, through whom are all things, and through whom we live." (1 Corinthians 8:6 - NKJV).

Paul reminds us that there is no other God but the one who created all things. There is one reality and one true God, the Father, who is the source of all creation and from whom we all derive life.

"one God and Father of all, who is above all, and through all, and in you all." (Ephesians 4:6 - NKJV).

The Father is the first member of the Godhead—He has taken the role of the Almighty God. Because no one word or name can describe the Infinite and Almighty God, He is known by many names.

2. What name is given to God the Father in Isaiah 9:6?

" ... and his name shall be called Wonderful, Counsellor, The mighty God, The everlasting Father, The Prince of Peace." (Isaiah 9:6b - KJV).

God, the Father, is called the everlasting Father by Isaiah. He is eternal. He existed in eternity-past, He exists now in the present, and will continue to exist in eternity-future. Note, in this verse, all the names listed for God also apply to the Son.

3. What name is given to God the Father in Daniel 7:13?

"I saw in the night visions, and, behold, one like the Son of man came with the clouds of heaven, and came to the Ancient of days, and they brought him near before him." (Daniel 7:13 - KJV).

God, the Father, is called the Ancient of Days. In Psalm 90:2, Moses said: *"Before the mountains were brought forth, or ever thou hadst formed the earth and the world, even from everlasting to everlasting, thou art God." (KJV).*

4. How does Daniel describe God the Father in Daniel 7:9?

"I beheld till the thrones were cast down, and the Ancient of days did sit, whose garment was white as snow, and the hair of his head like the pure wool: his throne was like the fiery flame, and his wheels as burning fire." (Daniel 7:9 - KJV).

God, the Father, is understood as being seated on the heavenly throne. He is in total control of the entire universe. Nothing happens without His knowledge and permission, and He remains on the throne continually. In the vision, Daniel saw the Father dressed in a snow-white garment with hair that was pure wool. This is almost identical to the description of Jesus in Revelation 1:13-14.

5. How does David describe God the Father in Psalm 103?

"The LORD is merciful and gracious, slow to anger, and abounding in mercy. But the mercy of the Lord is from everlasting to everlasting." (Psalm 103:8, 17a - NKJV).

Psalm 103 is a psalm of praise, sung in response to God's great love as experienced by David in his lifetime. On numerous occasions in his life of 70 years, he experienced the abundant mercies of God. Just as God, the Father, is eternal, so His mercies are everlasting.

6. *What kind of kingdom did God the Father establish?*

"The Lord has established His throne in heaven, and His kingdom rules over all." (Psalm 103:19 - NKJV)
The expression "throne in the heavens" denotes the eminence, glory, power, stability, and unchangeable nature of God's kingdom. The Sovereign made all, rules all creatures, both in heaven and earth, and does both by a word of power. God's firm and universal dominion is a pledge that He will keep His promises (see Psalm 11:4, Psalm 47:2, 8).[10]

"I know that whatever God does, it shall be forever. Nothing can be added to it, and nothing taken from it. God does it, that men should fear before Him." (Ecclesiastes 3:14 - NKJV).

7. *What can we learn about God the Father from Jesus' words in Luke 12:32?*

"Fear not, little flock; for it is your Father's good pleasure to give you the kingdom." (Luke 12:32 - KJV).

Our merciful and compassionate God delights in giving. He who gave us the gift of His Son wants to give us the gift of life in His kingdom.

---

[10] "Bible Commentary on Psalm 103:19",
https://biblehub.com/commentaries/psalms/103-19.htm

8. What is the kingdom of God like?

"Thy kingdom is an everlasting kingdom, and thy dominion endureth throughout all generations." (Psalm 145:13 - KJV).

" ... the kingdom of God is ... righteousness, ... peace, and joy in the Holy Ghost." (Romans 14:17 - KJV).

The kingdom of God is everlasting. It is also a kingdom of righteousness. All its citizens will live righteous lives and have peace and joy forever (see Psalm 16:11).

THE LESSON

The theme of Ecclesiastes 3 is all about God's timing. The Preacher knows that God, the Master Chef, will make everything beautiful in its appointed time. That means that God is in control and will make all things right again. In God's time, the world will experience healing, peace, deliverance, and renewed purpose.[11] It means we can trust God in our current season of life, whether in a calm or in a crisis, or somewhere in between.

God has put "eternity" or "the everlasting" in men's hearts, so there is a natural longing for unending life as well as the awareness that the beginning and the end of things are both beyond man's grasp.

The Preacher knows that only those things that are revealed to humanity about an eternal, infinite God can be understood. That's the reason the everlasting Father, the Alpha and Omega, the Beginning and the Ending (see Revelation 1:8) sent the Son to earth, to be a revelation of Himself (see Revelation 1:1).

---

[11] "What Does Ecclesiastes 3:11 Mean (He Has Made Everything Beautiful)", https://www.rethinknow.org/meaning-of-ecclesiastes-3-11/

THE TAKEAWAY

God, the Father, loved the world so much that He sent His One and only Son so that all who open their hearts and trust Jesus to heal their hearts will not perish but have everlasting life (see John 3:16) and live with Him in His kingdom and experience everlasting peace and joy (see Isaiah 51:11).

Personal Chef

"For wisdom is a defence, and money is a defence: but the excellency of knowledge is, that wisdom giveth life to them that have it." (Ecclesiastes 7:12 - KJV).

PERSONAL CHEF

- A personal chef usually cooks for a wide variety of clients. They may create a weekly menu that they'll prepare in large batches and deliver to their clients.[12]

I was once a customer of a company that offered a weekly lunch menu. There were two options: meat and meatless. I occasionally took advantage of their meatless offerings.

This study examines Jesus, personal Saviour.

1. Who is considered to be the second member of the Godhead?

"God, who at various times and in various ways spoke in time past to the fathers by the prophets, has in these last days spoken to us by His Son, whom He has appointed heir of all things, through whom also He made the worlds; who being the brightness of His glory and the express image of His person, and upholding all things by the word of His power, when He had by Himself purged our sins, sat down at the right hand of the Majesty on high." (Hebrews 1:1-3 - NKJV).

Jesus, the Son, is the second member of the Godhead. He is the embodiment or "the express image" of God, the Father. He came to

---

[12] "What Are The Culinary Arts?", https://www.escoffier.edu/blog/culinary-arts/what-are-the-culinary-arts/

the world as a personal Saviour to convey a message about God to His creation.

2. *What is the name given to the Son that tells us about His role?*

"Behold, a virgin shall be with child, and shall bring forth a son, and they shall call his name Emmanuel, which being interpreted is, God with us." (Matthew 1:23 - KJV).

The Son is the member of the Godhead who lives among God's creatures so that they can better understand what God is really like. The Son once lived and walked among the angels, and later, He came to earth and lived and walked among men. He is "Emmanuel," which means "God with us."

3. *What primary attribute of God the Father is revealed in Jesus?*

He that loveth not knoweth not God; for God is love. In this was manifested the love of God toward us, because that God sent his only begotten Son into the world, that we might live through him. (1 John 4:8-9 - KJV)

The revelation of God, the Father, in the person of Jesus Christ, is the central theme of John's gospel and the letters written by John and sent to the members of the early church. Jesus came to show us that God, the Father, loves us just as much and is just as kind and tender, just as loving and compassionate, merciful and forgiving as Jesus. Ultimately, God is love, and the Father Himself loves you!

4. In what role do we see the Son in Ephesians 3:9?

"and to make all see what is the fellowship of the mystery, which from the beginning of the ages has been hidden in God who created all things through Jesus Christ." (Ephesians 3:9 - NKJV).

The Son fulfils a significant role in relation to this world; He is Creator (see John 1:1-3,14 and Colossians 1:16-18).

5. What role do we see the Son taking in Nehemiah 9:6?

"You alone are the LORD; You have made heaven, the heaven of heavens, with all their host, the earth and everything on it, the seas and all that is in them, and You preserve them all. The host of heaven worships You. (Nehemiah 9:6 - NKJV).

According to this verse, the Son is the member of the Godhead through whom God created the earth. He is the Lord God in the Old Testament and the Lord Jesus Christ in the New Testament. He is the One who led the Israelites through the wilderness and gave the law on Mount Sinai (see Nehemiah 9:9-15).

That is what Paul had in mind when he said, *"For there is one God and one Mediator between God and men, the Man Christ Jesus."* (1 Timothy 2:5 - NKJV). The mediator is the Son. He is the link between heaven and earth; this has always been His role. We can't go up to heaven to God. God must come down to us, and the Son did that as Creator and Saviour. Christ is Saviour in the Old and New Testaments.

Jesus was sent that we, through Him, may lay hold on God and His gift of eternal life (see 1 Timothy 6:19), even as in the Son, the eternal Father lays hold on us.

34

6. *How is the message of God's love communicated in the life of Jesus?*

"For God so loved the world, that he gave his only begotten Son, that whosoever believeth in him should not perish, but have everlasting life." (John 3:16 - KJV).

"And we have seen and do testify that the Father sent the Son to be the Saviour of the world." (1 John 4:14 - KJV).

"And she shall bring forth a son, and thou shalt call his name JESUS: for he shall save his people from their sins." (Matthew 1:21 - KJV).

When it came to providing the ultimate truth about God to the human race, Jesus took on the characteristics of His creation. He came close to us so we could get the message about God clearly.

7. *What kind of kingdom did Jesus come to establish?*

"Jesus answered, My kingdom is not of this world:" (John 18:36a - KJV).

While on earth, Jesus did not accept an earthy throne to rule over the kingdoms of this world. He came to show us that the Father is love and that love is not selfish (see 1 Corinthians 13:5); love focuses on others (see Philippians 2:4-8). This could be likened to leaving His position as Chief Cook and becoming a mere bottlewasher in earth's kitchen.

THE LESSON

Ecclesiastes 7:11-12 reminds us that while wisdom and riches alike protect humanity from the storms and scorching heat of life, wisdom is by far superior. Financial wealth will not lengthen natural life, but true wisdom—the knowledge of God in Christ—will give spiritual life. Humanity's search for "something better" can only be satisfied by laying hold of the One whom to know is eternal life (see John 17:3).

Jesus shows us exactly what God is like in such a personal way that everyone can understand. That is the picture that we all need to see, and we see it perfectly in Jesus. This is why it is so important to study the life and teachings of Jesus in the Word of God. Then, one day, it will be said of us, *"as He is, so are we in this world"* (see 1 John 4:17).

THE TAKEAWAY

As a personal Chef, Jesus was no stranger to feeding multitudes. He who provided manna for the Israelites in the wilderness invites us to feed on the Bread of Life—who came down from heaven to give life to the world (see John 6:33-35). Won't you accept His offer today and live?

Private Chef

"If thou seest the oppression of the poor, and violent perverting of judgment and justice in a province, marvel not at the matter: for he that is higher than the highest regardeth; and there be higher than they." (Ecclesiastes 5:8 - KJV).

PRIVATE CHEF

- A private chef works for a single client or family, providing their daily meals. They might even live with the host family.[13]

The high school I attended was a boarding school. When I was in upper school, one of the privileges we had was access to the refrigerator in our house, which was located in my mother's room. I left my juices there periodically. There was just one problem with this arrangement. No one monitored the items that were removed from the refrigerator.

After my beverages were stolen a couple of times, I decided to do something to stop it. I prepared my usual beverage and added a little household bleach to the bottle, thinking this would somehow dissuade the perpetrator. Then, I could have the pleasure of enjoying my juices in peace.

Somehow, the housemother got wind of the bleach, and I got a stern reprimand. Her questions were, *"Did you not realise that you could harm someone? What drove you to do it? What next?"* My answers were, *"No,"* *"I wanted justice,"* and *"I'm sorry. I won't do it again."*

---

[13] "What Are The Culinary Arts?", https://www.escoffier.edu/blog/culinary-arts/what-are-the-culinary-arts/

This study examines some of the roles of the Holy Spirit, who operates much like a private chef.

1. *Who is the third member of the Godhead?*

"Go therefore and make disciples of all the nations, baptizing them in the name of the Father and of the Son and of the Holy Spirit." (Matthew 28:19 - NKJV)

God, the eternal Spirit, was present with the Father and the Son at Creation (see Genesis 1:3), was involved in the incarnation (see Luke 1:35), and works for the redemption of humanity (see Ephesians 4:30).

2. *According to John 14:16-18, what role will the Holy Spirit perform?*

"And I will pray the Father, and he shall give you another Comforter, that he may abide with you for ever; Even the Spirit of truth; whom the world cannot receive, because it seeth him not, neither knoweth him: but ye know him; for he dwelleth with you, and shall be in you. I will not leave you comfortless: I will come to you." (John 14:16-18 - KJV).

After Adam and Eve ate the forbidden fruit, they got scared, and when God approached them, they ran and hid from Him. God knew that they were afraid, so instead of sneaking up on them, He gently called out, *"Where are you?"* (see Genesis 3:9). Jesus usually reassured those around Him that there was no reason to be afraid of Him (see Matthew 14:27, Mark 6:50, Luke 24:39, John 6:20). God wants to soothe and comfort us. That is why the Holy Spirit is called the Comforter.

3. *According to John 15:26, what work will the Holy Spirit do?*

"But when the Comforter is come, whom I will send unto you from the Father, even the Spirit of truth, which proceedeth from the Father, he shall testify of me." (John 15:26 - KJV).

In an act of divine cooperation among the members of the Godhead, Jesus sent the Holy Spirit—the Spirit of Truth—from the Father to communicate to humanity a knowledge of something not known to them—Jesus' true purpose and mission. He expected that His disciples would continue to spread this message after he went back to be with His Father in heaven (see John 15:27).

4. *According to John 16:7-8, what roles will the Holy Spirit perform?*

"Nevertheless I tell you the truth; It is expedient for you that I go away: for if I go not away, the Comforter will not come unto you; but if I depart, I will send him unto you. And when he is come, he will reprove the world of sin, and of righteousness, and of judgment." (John 16:7-8 - KJV).

The Holy Spirit will make the people of the world conscious of sin, of righteousness, and of being judged.

- *Of sin:*

God's lovingkindness, forbearance, and goodness bring a consciousness of sin and lead to repentance (see Romans 2:4) and acceptance of the gospel—the good news of salvation (see Mark 1:15).

- *Of righteousness:*

When we read the Scriptures, the Holy Spirit opens our eyes to understand the principles of righteousness (see John 14:26 and John 16:13).

- *Of judgment:*

The Holy Spirit helps those who study the Word of God to turn from darkness to light, from Satan's lies to truth (see Psalm 119:130 and Acts 26:18).

5. *Why is it important to receive the Holy Spirit?*

"For as many as are led by the Spirit of God, they are the sons of God." (Romans 8:14 - KJV).

The Holy Spirit confirms that those who are guided by the Spirit of God are the children of God. When we invite the Holy Spirit into our lives, the Spirit lives in us, comforts us, encourages us, heals our hearts from sin, and empowers us to live God's way by giving us spiritual gifts.

6. *What is the evidence that someone has received the Holy Spirit?*

"... the fruit of the Spirit is love, joy, peace, longsuffering, gentleness, goodness, faith, meekness, temperance ..." (Galatians 5:22-23 - KJV).

Those who are under the influence and leading of the Holy Spirit will bear the fruit of the Spirit.

7. According to Acts 1:8, what role will the Holy Spirit perform?

"But you shall receive power when the Holy Spirit has come upon you; and you shall be witnesses to Me in Jerusalem, and in all Judea and Samaria, and to the end of the earth." (Acts 1:8 - NKJV).

The Holy Spirit empowers believers to be witnesses for God in the world around them and prepares the hearts of those with whom they will share the Word of God. The impact of the presence of the Holy Spirit in the lives of those who preached and practiced the Word of God is evident throughout the book of Acts. **"And the Lord added to the church daily such as should be saved."** (Acts 2:47 - KJV).

8. What role do the angels play in the ministry of the Holy Spirit to humanity?

"Are they not all ministering spirits, sent forth to minister for them who shall be heirs of salvation?" (Hebrews 1:14 - KJV).

God will dispatch angels to support those who believe and claim His promises while they do His work (see Psalm 91:11-12).

THE LESSON

When I kept losing my beverages to theft, I decided to fix things myself. While I did not expect to have my drink returned to me, I thought that I could teach someone a lesson and be "comforted" over my loss. I had taken on the Holy Spirit's roles of convictor and comforter.

I did not think that I should leave the offender to God, who sees everything, never overlooks evil, and never condones wrong (see

Ecclesiastes 5:8). I did not know God enough to trust Him to work out the situation for both my good and the perpetrator's. I believe that in the process, I hurt myself more than any other person.

THE TAKEAWAY

There is great danger in ignoring the convictions of the Holy Spirit, whether of sin, of judgment, or of righteousness. Today, if you hear His voice calling you to give up some harmful practice, to be open to a new experience with God, or to do the right thing as instructed in the Word of God, open your heart and follow the leading of the Spirit of Truth.

EAT ...

"There is nothing better for a man, than that he should eat and drink, and that he should make his soul enjoy good in his labour. This also I saw, that it was from the hand of God."
(Ecclesiastes 2:24 - KJV).

A Culinary Masterpiece

"To every thing there is a season, and a time to every purpose under the heaven." (Ecclesiastes 3:1 - KJV).

WHAT ARE CULINARY ARTS?

- Culinary arts is a broad term that refers to the preparation, cooking, plating, presentation, and service of food. It applies to meals and their components—like appetisers, side dishes, and main courses—rather than desserts or breads.

- The culinary arts umbrella covers a wide spectrum of disciplines, including food science and nutrition, the quality of the ingredients, seasonality, flavours and textures, styling and colour on the plate.

- Culinarians are disciplined creatives who combine science and art to make something distinctive and provide a rich, multifaceted experience encompassing all of our senses.[14]

In the culinary arts, timing is everything. The first watch I remember owning as a child was a girl's "Timex" watch. It consisted of a smooth, blue leather band and a cute face. It told time perfectly and lasted for years! What joy would it bring if everything in life was just as reliable and dependable? This study focuses on creation.

---

[14] "What Are The Culinary Arts?", https://www.escoffier.edu/blog/culinary-arts/what-are-the-culinary-arts/

1. When did time on earth begin?

"A time to be born, and a time to die; a time to plant, and a time to pluck up that which is planted;" (Ecclesiastes 3:2 - KJV).

Solomon launched into a series of famous contrasts in Ecclesiastes 3 to let the reader know that there is a season and a time for everything under the sun (see verses 1 to 8). Ecclesiastes 3:2 speaks of *"a time to be born, and a time to die; a time to plant, and a time to pluck up that which is planted."*

Time on earth began after the members of the Godhead counseled together and made the decision to create earth. It was a glorious, miraculous, exciting time—a time of new beginnings.

2. Which member of the Godhead took on the role of Creator of this world?

"In the beginning was the Word, and the Word was with God, and the Word was God. He was in the beginning with God. All things were made through Him, and without Him nothing was made that was made." (John 1:1-3 - NKJV).

"And to make all men see what is the fellowship of the mystery, which from the beginning of the world hath been hid in God, who created all things by Jesus Christ." (Ephesians 3:9 - KJV).

"For by him were all things created, that are in heaven, and that are in earth, visible and invisible, whether they be thrones, or dominions, or principalities, or powers: all things were created by him, and for him: And he is before all things, and by him all things consist." (Colossians 1:16-17 - KJV).

The previous passages confirm that Jesus, the Son, took on a significant role as Creator of this world.

3. *Who witnessed the creation of earth?*

"Where were you when I laid the foundation of the earth? … when the morning stars sang together and all the sons of Elohim shouted for joy? (Job 38:4, 7 – NOG).

In response to the work of creation, the morning stars—the angels of God—sang together, and the sons of Elohim shouted with joy (see Job 38:4-6). Revelation 1:20 refers to the seven stars as the seven angels of the seven churches. The term "sons of Elohim" is understood to mean the heads or rulers of other planets (distant worlds … apart from earth) that God had created (see Job 1:6-7, John 12:31).

4. *How long did the earth's creation take?*

"And on the seventh day God ended his work which he had made …" (Genesis 2:2a - KJV).

The creation of our world took seven days. On each day of creation week, something different was done. The Hebrew word for day in Genesis 1 and 2 is "yom"; a word which means a literal 24-hour day.

5. *What did God do in the creation week? (Read Job 38 and 39).*

"In the beginning God created the heavens and the earth." (Genesis 1:1 - NKJV).

Acts of God in the week of earth's creation included laying the foundation or base of earth, putting in the lines of the equator, designing the clouds, setting boundaries for the sea, and establishing the law of gravity. At that time, storehouses were reserved for snow, and constellations were set in place. In that week, the environment for the sustenance of life on earth was put in place.

6. *What does the sequence of creation tell us about God? (Read Genesis 1:1-31).*

"Let all things be done decently and in order." (1 Corinthians 14:40 - KJV).

When God created our world and everything in it in six days, He did it in an orderly way, with three days of forming and three days of filling. He started by forming empty shapes:

- Day one: light.
- Day two: the oceans and the sky.
- Day three: dry ground and plants.

Then, after He had created these beautiful templates of space, God began to fill the empty shapes with His creative masterpieces.

- Day four: God filled the light with the sun, moon and stars.
- Day five: He filled the oceans and sky with marine life and birds.
- Day six: He filled the ground with animals and his crowning act of creation—intelligent people created in His image.

7. What was God's final act at the end of the creation week?

"Thus the heavens and the earth, and all the host of them, were finished. And on the seventh day God ended His work which He had done, and He rested on the seventh day from all His work which He had done. Then God blessed the seventh day and sanctified it, because in it He rested from all His work which God had created and made." (Genesis 2:1-3 - NKJV).

The creation of the sabbath by Jesus, the Lord of the Sabbath (see Matthew 12:8), was like an artist putting the finishing signature on a beautiful painting. In doing this, He established the sabbath as a perpetual memorial of His completed created work.

THE LESSON

The creation of earth was not a random event. In the same way that a culinary expert will carefully plan the next masterpiece on the menu for his guests and a watch-maker must use an intelligent design to make a watch that will function properly, God's act of creation was a carefully planned event to set the perfect physical environment in place for the sustenance of the first family and their offspring.

God always works in this orderly, deliberate way. He always thinks ahead, plans ahead, and prepares us for what He is doing. Just as He brought order out of chaos in the creation of the world, He alone can bring order from chaos in the re-creation of our hearts and minds.

THE TAKEAWAY

Perhaps right now, you are experiencing a new beginning on this journey of life. Know that you can trust the Creator of all things with your life's outcome.

Forbidden Fruit

"Truly, this only I have found: That God made man upright, but they have sought out many schemes." (Ecclesiastes 7:29 - NKJV).

DID YOU KNOW?

- While the broad definition of culinary arts may imply that it includes the preparation of ALL foods, industry professionals usually separate culinary from baking and pastry.

- The difference is generally attributed to the way the two arts are approached. In culinary arts, the recipes can often be open to interpretation and tweaks made on the fly—a little extra salt, a slightly longer cooking time.

- In baking and pastry, each recipe has a scientific formula that must be followed to the letter. It's much more precise and, therefore, does not allow for the same kind of adjustments as the culinary arts.[15]

I learnt from my friend, Tamara, that cooking is an art and baking is a science. She is good at both. Believe me, her curried chickpeas and breadfruit make a delicious breakfast!

In the previous study, we learnt that the members of the Godhead put great thought into the creation of our world. It wasn't a random accident. There was a grand design. In this study, we will take a close look at the creation of humanity.

---

[15] "What Are The Culinary Arts?", https://www.escoffier.edu/blog/culinary-arts/what-are-the-culinary-arts/

1. *What was God's grand plan for the creation of humanity?*

" Then Elohim said, "Let us make humans in our image, in our likeness. … So Elohim created humans in his image. In the image of Elohim he created them. He created them male and female." *(Genesis 1:26a-27 – NOG).*

"This is the book of the genealogy of Adam. In the day that God created man, He made him in the likeness of God. He created them male and female, and blessed them and called them Mankind in the day they were created." (Genesis 5:1-2 - NKJV).

God's desire was that humanity would reflect His image (function as representatives of the Godhead) and His likeness (model His attributes and His character). Being created in God's image means that Adam and Eve had purpose in life. They were created to reflect the glory or the character of their Creator.

2. *What was the position of the human family in God's Creation?*

"Yet you have made him a little lower than the heavenly beings and crowned him with glory and honor." (Psalm 8:5 - ESV).

Adam and Eve were created with superior mental powers and the ability to reason with their Creator. They were given liberty to make intelligent choices. Adam was given the task of naming the beasts of the field and the birds of the air (see Genesis 2:19-20).

3. *According to Genesis 1:26b, 28, why did God create the first family?*

"Let them rule the fish in the sea, the birds in the sky, the domestic animals all over the earth, and all the animals that crawl on the

earth. … Elohim blessed them and said, "Be fertile, increase in number, fill the earth, and be its master. Rule the fish in the sea, the birds in the sky, and all the animals that crawl on the earth." (Genesis 1:26b, 28 – NOG).

- *Parents:*

Adam and Eve were given the capacity to have children who shared their attributes. If they remained faithful to their purpose to reflect the glory of God, their children would also reflect the image and likeness of the Creator.

- *Stewards:*

They were also created to have dominion over the rest of God's creation—they were expected to care for the earth's physical environment and for the other creatures that God had made (see Psalm 8:6-8).

4. *How did God feel about the creation of the first family?*

"And Elohim saw everything that he had made and that it was very good. There was evening, then morning—the sixth day." (Genesis 1:31 – NOG).

After He created Adam and Eve in His image on day six of creation week, God announced that everything that He had created was very good. God was very pleased with His original design.

5. *What was the process by which God created man?*

"And the LORD God formed man of the dust of the ground, and breathed into his nostrils the breath of life; and man became a living being." (Genesis 2:7 - NKJV).

51

Before God breathed His breath of life into Adam, there was no life in man. The same divine power that was used to inspire the Word of God (see 2 Timothy 3:16), to form and to fill the creation (see Genesis 1:3, 6, 9, 11, 14, 20, 24), also provided the life-giving spark in man (see Genesis 1:26, 28, 29).

6. *What command did God give to Adam in Eden?*

"Yahweh Elohim commanded the man. He said, "You are free to eat from any tree in the garden. But you must never eat from the tree of the knowledge of good and evil because when you eat from it, you will certainly die."" (Genesis 2:16-17 – NOG).

Mankind was meant to live forever and enjoy a harmonious relationship with their Creator. Adam and Eve were given the gift of conditional immortality. The condition on which they would be granted eternal life was conformity to the nature and will of God for man—adherence to the Creator's law of love and liberty. Any violation of this law would result in a loss of their rich blessings.

7. *What impact did Adam and Eve's choice to go against the will of God have on their offspring?*

"And Adam lived one hundred and thirty years, and begot a son in his own likeness, after his image, and named him Seth." (Genesis 5:3 - NKJV).

"For what happens to the sons of men also happens to animals; one thing befalls them: as one dies, so dies the other. Surely, they all have one breath; man has no advantage over animals, for all is vanity." (Ecclesiastes 3:19 - NKJV).

As a result of Adam and Eve's choice to go against the principle of obedience to God's Word and to eat of the Tree of the Knowledge of Good and Evil, they lost their gift of immortality and became subject to death (see Genesis 3:19) and so did their children born in Adam's likeness (see Romans 5:12). Their previously pleasurable work became challenging (see Genesis 3:17-18), and they lost their place in their garden home (see Genesis 3:24).

THE LESSON

When Solomon tried to obtain knowledge of sin and to understand how worldly things worked, *"to know the wickedness of folly, even of foolishness and madness"* (see Ecclesiastes 7:25) and to find pleasure in the same way that those around him did, in loving many strange women (see Ecclesiastes 7:26), he found that he was left empty and unfulfilled (see Ecclesiastes 7:28). He sought out many inventions [devices or schemes] (see Ecclesiastes 7:29). These devices were ways of deviating from original righteousness. For much of the book of Ecclesiastes, he called the experiences gained from indulging in the pleasures of this world "vanity and vexation of spirit."

According to Benson's Bible Commentary, our first parents were made mentally "upright"; they were morally innocent before God with the desire to do God's will and to please Him. Adam and Eve, and their children after them, sought out many inventions. They were not content with their current state but studied new ways of making themselves wiser and happier than God had made them. We, their wretched children, are still prone to forsake the certain rule of God's Word and the true way of happiness and to seek new methods of attaining it.

THE TAKEAWAY

Humanity was blessed with the gift of creativity, enabling us to use art and science to create things that uplift humanity. True happiness is found in the ways of God. Seeking wisdom and happiness outside of this safety zone results in destruction. Let us seek the Lord so we may live.

DRINK ...

"… every man should eat and drink and enjoy the good of all his labor—it is the gift of God." (Ecclesiastes 3:13 - NKJV).

The War in Heaven

"Wisdom is better than weapons of war: but one sinner destroys much good." (Ecclesiastes 9:18 - NKJV).

WHAT DO ALL BREADS HAVE IN COMMON?

- At the most basic level, bread baking consists of cooking a mixture of milled grains with water. Raised breads involve the complex interactions between flour and the leaveners that give them their porous, tender quality.[16]

- Leaveners come in two main forms: baking powder or baking soda and yeast. Baking powder and baking soda are used to leaven baked goods that have a delicate structure, ones that rise quickly as carbon dioxide is produced, such as quick breads like cornbread and biscuits.[17]

It is not uncommon to associate war with physical weapons such as guns and bombs. As a child, I developed a mental picture of how a war tank looked, although I had never seen one before. Quite likely, it sprang from a book I read from the public library near home or one that my mother's cousins gave me as a birthday or Christmas gift.

THE GREAT CONTROVERSY - A TIMELESS WAR

The books of Isaiah and Ezekiel in the Old Testament and Revelation—the last book of the New Testament—provide

---

[16] "Bread Science 101" https://www.exploratorium.edu/explore/cooking/bread-science

[17] "Activity: Yeast-Air Balloons", https://annex.exploratorium.edu/cooking/bread/activity-yeast.html

glimpses into a war that began in heaven and is still raging on earth today. This study explores this war in heaven and its implications for us.

1. *What is the origin of evil?*

"For thou hast said in thine heart, I will ascend into heaven, I will exalt my throne above the stars of God [El]: I will sit also upon the mount of the congregation, in the sides of the north: I will ascend above the heights of the clouds; I will be like the most High." (Isaiah 14:13-14 - KJV).

"'This is what Adonay Yahweh says: You think you are wise like Elohim. ... Your behavior was perfect from the time you were created, until evil was found in you." (Ezekiel 28:6,15 – NOG).

Lucifer—a beautiful angel created by God—became jealous of and coveted the esteemed position of the Son of God in the government and leadership council of God. Jesus reasoned with him, showing him the error of his ways, but he refused to concede.

2. *Where did the war in heaven begin?*

"And there was war in heaven: Michael and his angels fought against the dragon; and the dragon fought and his angels." (Revelation 12:7 - KJV).

Lucifer, hiding his ill-feelings towards Christ and his secret fantasy of being Elohim (Creator), promoted his evil and rebellious thoughts about God among the angels in heaven, and soon enough, discontent began to foment like the effect of baking soda working in flour.

3. Who else was drawn into the war in heaven?

"How art thou fallen from heaven, O Lucifer, son of the morning! how art thou cut down to the ground, which didst weaken the nations!" (Isaiah 14:12 - KJV).

"His tail drew a third of the stars of heaven and threw them to the earth ..." (Revelation 12:4 - NKJV).

This hostility eventually bubbled over into open rebellion, and he tricked a significant number of the angels in heaven into taking his side in a war of ideas and words, attacking the law, government, and the character of God (especially His fairness).

4. What weapons were used in the war in heaven?

"By thy great wisdom and by thy traffick hast thou increased thy riches, and thine heart is lifted up because of thy riches. ... Thou hast defiled thy sanctuaries by the multitude of thine iniquities, by the iniquity of thy traffick ..." (Ezekiel 28:5, 18 - KJV).

According to Webster's 1828 Dictionary, trafficking means "trading; bartering; buying and selling goods, wares and commodities." Satan went around peddling lies. This was his primary weapon, and he became known as the father of lies (see John 8:44). Other powerful weapons that were used in this war include innuendo, flattery, arguments, and trickery.

5. What was the result of the war in heaven?

" ... Michael and his angels fought against the dragon; and the dragon fought and his angels. And prevailed not; neither was their place found any more in heaven. And the great dragon was cast out, that old serpent, called the Devil, and Satan, which

deceiveth the whole world: he was cast out into the earth, and his angels were cast out with him." (Revelation 12:7-9 - KJV).

"How art thou fallen from heaven, O Lucifer, son of the morning! how art thou cut down to the ground, which didst weaken the nations!" (Isaiah 14:12 - KJV).

Consequently, Satan and the angels who fell for his lies were expelled from the courts of heaven.

6. *What made Satan so effective in the war in heaven?*

"Thou art the anointed cherub that covereth; and I have set thee so: thou wast upon the holy mountain of God; thou hast walked up and down in the midst of the stones of fire." (Ezekiel 28:14 - KJV).

Satan's strategy was effective because he misused his elevated position as the covering cherub—having direct access to the throne of God—to promote his evil, hidden agenda of undermining God's government and authority. Being known for his proximity to the throne of God, he was considered to be trustworthy. He deceived about one-third of the angels in heaven (see Revelation 12:4) into believing his lies about the nature of the law of God and God's character. He suggested that the angels did not need God to tell them how to live but that they could govern themselves well enough.

THE LESSON

Satan's example confirms what the Preacher said in Ecclesiastes 9:18, *"Wisdom is better than weapons of war: but one sinner destroys much good."* **(KJV).** According to Barnes Notes on the Bible, the word "sinner" in the original language indicates intellectual as well as moral error.

Bad counsel or ideas tend to travel further and have a greater impact than physical weapons in armed combat. The effects of evil counsel may bring much damage to the talebearer himself and mischief to others, which could last a lifetime and impact countless generations.

In the childhood game of Chinese telephone, where a message is passed along from person to person, what started out as a clear instruction often came out sounding quite different from the original.

Distortion along the communication lines and disruption of the perfection in heaven can be laid squarely at Satan's feet. Due to pride, Lucifer, a perfectly created being, became Satan—God's adversary—and, by his evil counsel, led a portion of the angels of heaven into rebellion against God in a war of words.

THE TAKEAWAY

Even perfect beings can be led astray if they believe lies about the character, government, and law of God. The only safeguard against Satan's lies is true knowledge and correct understanding of the holy Scriptures, which testify of God.

The War on Earth

"Dead flies cause the ointment of the apothecary to send forth a stinking savour: so doth a little folly him that is in reputation for wisdom and honour." (Ecclesiastes 10:1 - KJV).

DID YOU KNOW?

- In 1857, Louis Pasteur discovered that yeast is a living organism and that its activity causes fermentation.[18]

- This organism lies dormant until it comes into contact with warm water. Once reactivated, yeast begins feeding on the sugars in flour and releases the carbon dioxide that makes bread rise (although at a much slower rate than baking powder or baking soda).[19]

After he was evicted from heaven with the angels who followed him in rebelling against the Creator, Satan took the fight to earth, where he started a conversation with Eve in her Edenic garden home. This study focuses on the war on earth.

1. *What weapons are used in the war on earth?*

"The snake was more clever than all the wild animals Yahweh Elohim had made. He asked the woman, "Did Elohim really say, 'You must never eat the fruit of any tree in the garden'?" ... "You certainly won't die!" the snake told the woman. "Elohim knows

---

[18] "Activity: Yeast-Air Balloons",
https://annex.exploratorium.edu/cooking/bread/activity-yeast.html

[19] "Bread Science 101", https://www.exploratorium.edu/explore/cooking/bread-science

that when you eat it your eyes will be opened. You'll be like Elohim, knowing good and evil.""" (Genesis 3:1, 4, 5 – NOG).

- *Distraction*

Eve took the first step on her downward journey when she wandered away from her safe place in Adam's company. Her decision took her into Satan's enchanted ground at the Tree of the Knowledge of Good and Evil.

- *Doubt*

As he had opportunity, Satan first cast a cloud of doubt over the words God had spoken to Adam in Genesis 2:16-17. He did so by questioning Eve concerning the truth that God had already made abundantly clear to the first family regarding the consequences of eating from the Tree of the Knowledge of Good and Evil (see Genesis 3:1).

- *Distrust*

The Devil insinuated that God was a liar and was hiding "the good stuff"—knowledge of evil—from the first family. Satan always tries to twist the truth, to make evil seem good and good seem evil in order to get us to distrust God. He tried this trick with Jesus during the temptation in the wilderness (see Matthew 4:1-11).

His end is sure, **"Woe unto them that call evil good, and good evil; that put darkness for light, and light for darkness; that put bitter for sweet, and sweet for bitter!" (Isaiah 5:20 – KJV).**

- *Deception*

As Eve's dialogue with the Devil progressed, he told the biggest lie of all, convincing Eve that eating the fruit of disobedience would not result in death (see Genesis 3:4). Satan also went on to imply that his way, that is, having knowledge of evil, was better than God's way (see Genesis 3:5).

Satan's lies operate like yeast on sugar. He is very effective when there is some "flour" in our lives to feed on, such as unresolved childhood trauma and broken relationships. He has been "leavening" the minds of those who would linger in his presence long enough to listen to his lies about God, repackaging evil and attacking truth with much success ever since Eden (see 1 Peter 5:8).

2. *What are some modern-day manifestations of the war on earth?*

"And no marvel; for Satan himself is transformed into an angel of light. Therefore it is no great thing if his ministers also be transformed as the ministers of righteousness; whose end shall be according to their works." (2 Corinthians 11:14-15 - KJV).

Satan engages in the war on earth directly himself or through his agents. Satanic agents include evil angels and human ministers of unrighteousness.

- *Arch-enemy*

Satan attended to the temptation of Jesus himself. His objective was to get the Son of God, the Creator of the angels, to bow down and worship him, a created being (see Matthew 4:9-10). Had this worked, the plan of salvation would have been destroyed, and humanity would be doomed forever.

- *Angels*

Just as Satan used the medium of a serpent in Eden to trick Eve into partaking of the forbidden fruit, his fallen angels are going around the earth on a mission to seduce humanity—the apple of God's eye (see Zechariah 2:8)—into dishonouring God's Word and breaking God's law.

His devices will include using fallen angels to impersonate dead loved ones in an attempt to deliver false messages, presumably from God (see 1 Samuel 28).

In 1 Samuel 28, God's prophet Samuel had died and King Saul had stopped receiving messages from the LORD. Saul consulted a medium in an attempt to get a word from "God." This was necromancy, attempting to communicate with the dead, a practice that was expressly forbidden by God (see Deuteronomy 18:11). At this consultation, the woman said to Saul, "I saw a spirit ascending out of the earth" (see 1 Samuel 28:13 – NKJV). The Hebrew word used here is "elohiym", rendered "gods" in the KJV.

According to Barnes' Notes on the Bible[20], elohiym is used in 1 Samuel 28:13 in a general sense of a supernatural appearance, either **angel** or spirit. Texts in the Bible such as Ecclesiastes 9:5 and Psalm 146:4 state that "the dead know nothing" and in the day that someone dies, "his thoughts perish" – they die with him.

According to Matthew Poole's Commentary[21], on 1 Samuel 28:14, while it appeared that Saul got a prophetic word from Samuel, this was based on the medium's representation and Saul's perception. Why would God, who had just refused to answer Saul by the means

---

[20] BibleHub.com

[21] BibleHub.com

which He had appointed, now use means which he, God, detested? The fact that this spirit accepts worship from a man (another thing forbidden by God – see Revelation 19:10) is telltale that it was not an angelic messenger from God but an evil angel or evil spirit.

- *Agents*

Satan used Eve to tempt Adam to partake of the forbidden fruit (see Genesis 3:6). He will stop at nothing in his bid to destroy humanity—including using loved ones who are alive—because he knows his days are numbered (see Revelation 12:12).

In the church, he will continue to play his trump card of "accusing the brethren" (see Revelation 12:10), similar to how Adam accused Eve in Eden (see Genesis 3:12).

- *"Acts of God"*

Satan also works through the inanimate objects of God's creation to wreak havoc and cause mayhem while casting the blame on God for his destructive actions, such as fires and tornadoes (see Job 1:16,19).

THE LESSON

According to Barnes Notes on the Bible[22], an apothecary was a dealer in spices and perfumes (see Exodus 30:25). The swarms of flies in the East would corrupt and destroy any moist unguent or mixture left uncovered and pollute a dish of food in a few minutes.

Dead flies in the ointment, no matter how small, tend to result in the swift destruction of a mixture and could be very costly. All sin has

---

[22] BibleHub.com

big consequences, whether the results are immediately apparent or not. The ultimate outcome is death if there is no remedy.

Eve was led down the road to death by several small actions. From being out of position, to yielding to Satan's doubtful suggestions, to engaging in dialogue and debate with him, she was seduced into becoming a seductress herself, luring her beloved Adam into the Devil's well-laid trap.

THE TAKEAWAY

One thing that everyone living on earth will experience is the results of sin. We will all be called to choose a side in the battle of good against evil, of Christ versus Satan; to live in the kingdom of God and be subjected to His holy, just, and good law (see Romans 7:12), and his authority (see Romans 12:1), or to be confirmed to the kingdom of evil and the principles of the Devil (see Romans 12:2).

Those who yield to the lies told by Satan will one day turn against God and His people. The righteous are assured by the promises in Psalm 37:25 and Isaiah 33:16 that in the day of adversity and times of trouble, their bread and water will be sure and that good angels will cover them (see Psalm 91:12).

"No Thank You."

"A time to rend, and a time to sew; a time to keep silence, and a time to speak." (Ecclesiastes 3:7 - KJV).

DID YOU KNOW?

- In addition to carbon dioxide, yeast also produces alcohol as it feeds on sugar, which is why it is an important ingredient in making beer. Beer froth has a long history as a source of yeast. It was used to leaven bread both in ancient Egypt and in nineteenth-century England.[23]

- Beer foam, also known as barm or ale yeast, was collected from the top of fermenting beer and used to leaven bread. A barm cake is a soft, round bread roll from North West England that is traditionally leavened with barm. In Ireland, barm is used in the traditional production of barmbrack, a fruit bread.[24]

This study focuses on Jesus' life, death, and resurrection.

JESUS' LIFE

1. *What was Jesus' first miracle? (Read John 2:1-9).*

"When the ruler of the feast had tasted the water that was made wine..." (John 2:9 – KJV).

---

[23] "Activity: Yeast-Air Balloons",
https://annex.exploratorium.edu/cooking/bread/activity-yeast.html

[24] "Barm", https://en.m.wikipedia.org/wiki/Barm#:~:

The first recorded miracle performed by Jesus was to turn plain water into wine at a wedding in Cana.

2. What was the nature of this miracle wine?

"When the ruler of the feast tasted the water now become wine, and didn't know where it came from (but the servants who had drawn the water knew), the ruler of the feast called the bridegroom and said to him, "Everyone serves the good wine first, and when the guests have drunk freely, then that which is worse. You have kept the good wine until now!" (John 2:9-10 - KJV).

This wine was commended by the host for being better than the wine previously offered to the guests. Based on the internal consistencies of Scripture, (Proverbs 20:1 (KJV) – **"Wine is a mocker, strong drink is raging: and whosoever is deceived thereby is not wise. "**, it is understood that the wine that was miraculously provided by Christ for the feast was unfermented wine, the fruit of the vine, or non-alcoholic grape juice. Isaiah calls it the new wine in the cluster in Isaiah 65:8.

3. What was the wine symbolic of?

"Forasmuch as ye know that ye were not redeemed with corruptible things, as silver and gold, from your vain conversation received by tradition from your fathers; But with the precious blood of Christ, as of a lamb without blemish and without spot." (1 Peter 1:18-19 - KJV).

This wine was a symbol of Jesus' own blood, which was to be shed for the sins of the world. At the Passover supper, the emblems of the unleavened cakes and the unfermented wine were symbolic of the unblemished sacrifice of Jesus, the *"Lamb without blemish and without spot."*

Jesus fulfilled several Old Testament prophecies in His life and in His death.

4. *What prophecy did Jesus fulfil while on trial?*

"He was oppressed, and he was afflicted, yet he opened not his mouth: he is brought as a lamb to the slaughter, and as a sheep before her shearers is dumb, so he openeth not his mouth." *(Isaiah 53:7 - KJV).*

- *A Time To Speak*

When Jesus stood before the governor (Pilate), the governor asked him, "Are you the King of the Jews?" He answered, "It is as you say" or "You have spoken the truth" (see Matthew 27:11). Jesus did not deny the implied title of "Messiah" or "Saviour."

- *A Time to Be Silent*

When He was accused by the chief priests and elders, he said nothing (see Matthew 27:12). When Pilate said unto him, "Hearest thou not how many things they witness against thee?" He said nothing (see Matthew 27:13-14). He bore all these false accusations in silence, making no effort to defend Himself.

"Christ holds his peace when he is accused in order that we may not be accused: acknowledging our guiltiness, and at the same time, His own innocence.[25]

---

[25] Geneva Study Bible Commentary - BibleHub.com

5. *What prophecy was fulfilled while Jesus hung on the cross?*

"Reproach hath broken my heart; and I am full of heaviness: and I looked for some to take pity, but there was none; and for comforters, but I found none." (Psalm 69:20 - KJV).

Satan used passers-by to say bitter words to Jesus (see Matthew 27:39-40), he used the chief priests, scribes and elders to mock him (see Matthew 27:41-42), and even the two thieves on their crosses on His left and right sides—who themselves were condemned to death—said evil words to the One who gave His life for the salvation of the people of the world (see Matthew 27:44).

According to Barnes' Notes on the Bible[26], "at first both" of the thieves reviled Jesus, but afterward, one of them relented and became penitent, perhaps from witnessing the patient sufferings of Christ.

6. *What is the symbolism of the fulfilment of Psalm 69:21 recorded in Matthew 27:34?*

"They gave me also gall for my meat; and in my thirst they gave me vinegar to drink." (Psalm 69:21 - KJV).

"They gave him vinegar to drink mingled with gall: and when he had tasted thereof, he would not drink." (Matthew 27:34 - KJV).

It was customary to give those who suffered death by way of the cross something to deaden their pain. In keeping with the tradition of the day, when Jesus hung on the cross, He was offered a mixture

---

[26] BibleHub.com

of vinegar or sour wine mixed with bitter gall to dull the pain of His crucifixion. This was a direct fulfilment of the prophecy in Psalm 69:21. In response, He said, "No thank you" (my paraphrase).

Accepting this pain-numbing drug would have dulled his senses at a time when He most needed to be alert to the distractions of Satan.

JESUS' RESURRECTION

7. *What prophecy did Jesus fulfil while in the grave?*

"I am your chosen one. You won't leave me in the grave or let my body decay." (Psalm 16:10 - CEV).

"That he should still live for ever, and not see corruption." (Psalm 49:9 - KJV).

The Scriptures had predicted that Christ, the Holy One, the Bread of Life (see John 6:35), would not be left in the grave to see corruption (decay) (see Psalm 16:10, Psalm 49:9, Acts 2:27,31, and Acts 13:35). In fulfilment of this prophecy, Jesus was resurrected to sit on the throne of God (see Acts 2:30, 32 and 2 Corinthians 13:4).

8. *What prophecy did Jesus fulfil when He was resurrected?*

" ... he taught his disciples, and said unto them, the Son of man is delivered into the hands of men, and they shall kill him; and after that he is killed, he shall rise the third day. But they understood not that saying, and were afraid to ask him. (Mark 9:31-32 - KJV).

"Then opened he their understanding, that they might understand the scriptures, and said unto them, thus it is written, and thus it

behoved Christ to suffer, and to rise from the dead the third day."
(Luke 24:45-46 - KJV).

The timing of Jesus' resurrection fulfils His own predictions and aligns with the Jewish concept of "three days" as a period of significant transformation or divine intervention. It underscores the precision and reliability of God's plan as revealed in Scripture.

THE LESSON

When Jesus stood before His accusers, He had an interesting array of conversations. He knew when it was time to keep silent and when it was time to speak (see Ecclesiastes 3:1).

His followers will also be persecuted for their faith (see 2 Timothy 3:12). When this happens, they need not worry about what to say. The right words will be impressed upon their minds by the Holy Spirit when they are needed (see Matthew 10:19).

Those who partake of Christ's sufferings, like Stephen, Paul, and Peter (see Acts 7:59, Acts 9:23, and 1 Peter 1:6-7), will also partake of His glory when He shall "sit upon the throne of His glory" (see Matthew 19:28-29). "Because He lives, we shall live also" (see John 14:19).

THE TAKEAWAY

Because Jesus is Lord and Christ (see Acts 2:36), His followers can look forward to the day when they will see the One who lived and died for them and then rose in victory to sit on God's throne. When this is realised, it will be a time of joyous celebration, when believers in Jesus' life, death, and resurrection—having left all the pain and shame of the past behind them—will live with Jesus in His Father's kingdom for all eternity. Oh, what a glorious day that will be!

The Water of Life

"A time to be born, and a time to die; a time to plant, and a time to pluck up that which is planted." (Ecclesiastes 3:2 - KJV).

DID YOU KNOW?

- One of the herbs that I am familiar with from the backyard at my childhood home is black sage. As children, we learnt that the black sage plant was great for oral hygiene when used as a chewstick. I was happy to find it growing in my backyard recently.

- Sage Salvia Officinalis, or sage, is an unsung heroine of our spice cabinets. This lack of favour might be due to its astringent taste, but this plant held center stage in ancient times. Its power is evident, even in its name—salvia means "to save" in Greek.

- This culinary herb is so drying that nursing mothers are advised to use this tea if they want to cease milk production. For some, this same astringing power makes sage their number one remedy when working with sore, swollen throats.

- It can be used in a throat spray, a gargle, or a tea with honey and lemon. Used as a mouth rinse, sage is wonderful for all inflammation of gums and the mouth. Our elders knew this!

- Highly aromatic, sage contains antioxidants and other compounds that support immune function when working against microbes. It has been used for centuries to promote memory and cognitive health.[27]

This study explores the experience of salvation.

1. What is salvation?

"Heal me, O LORD, and I shall be healed; save me, and I shall be saved: for thou art my praise." (Jeremiah 17:14 - KJV).

One Greek word for salvation is "sōtēria." It means "to deliver health." In a nutshell, salvation is healing. In Jeremiah 17:14, we see that the words salvation and healing can be interchanged.

2. Who needs salvation?

"The heart is deceitful above all things, and desperately wicked: who can know it?" (Jeremiah 17:9 - KJV).

Humanity is spiritually sick—terminally ill—and without intervention from Someone who can heal us, the entire human race will naturally self-destruct. This spiritual heart disease is a disease of the mind. It is reflected in the damage done to our way of thinking. It moves from having righteous thoughts to having wicked, rebellious thoughts.

Consider Adam and Eve in Eden. They made up their minds that God could not be trusted and chose to believe Satan's lies instead of God's Word. They passed on this selfish, distrustful, brain-damaging attitude to their offspring, and we have been experiencing

---

[27] "Medicinal Uses for 8 Herbs Already In Your Kitchen"
https://www.chelseagreen.com/2024/medicinal-uses-for-8-herbs-already-in-your-kitchen/#:

the results in our world ever since (see Romans 5:12 and James 1:15).

3. Who can heal?

"I the LORD search the heart, I try the reins, even to give every man according to his ways, and according to the fruit of his doings." (Jeremiah 17:10 - KJV).

The God who created all (see Colossians 1:16-17) is also the author and finisher of our faith (see Hebrews 12:2). Jesus is the great Master Chef who invites us to experience the joys of salvation, to taste and see that the LORD is good, and to receive the healing blessings that come from trusting in Him (see Psalm 34:8).

4. What is our part in salvation's plan?

"And be not conformed to this world: but be ye transformed by the renewing of your mind, that ye may prove what is that good, and acceptable, and perfect, will of God." (Romans 12:2 - KJV).

In the experience of salvation, God does the work of saving us. Our responsibility is to allow God to change us. We can rest in the promise that He who began a good work in us will be faithful to complete it (see Philippians 1:6). We can trust Him to give us new hearts, to change our way of thinking, and to shape a new life in us from the inside out (see Jeremiah 31:33-34).

5. What are the steps to salvation?

"If we say that we have no sin, we deceive ourselves, and the truth is not in us. If we confess our sins, he is faithful and just to forgive us our sins, and to cleanse us from all unrighteousness." (1 John 1:8-9 - KJV).

"My little children, these things write I unto you, that ye sin not. And if any man sin, we have an advocate with the Father, Jesus Christ the righteous: And he is the propitiation for our sins: and not for our's only, but also for the sins of the whole world. And hereby we do know that we know him, if we keep his commandments." (1 John 2:1-3 - KJV).

We must:

1. Admit that we are sick (see 1 John 1:8).
2. Access a trustworthy Physician (see 1 John 2:1).
3. Approach the Healer (see 1 John 1:9).
4. Always keep our appointments (see 1 John 2:3).
5. Apply our medicine (see 1 John 1:7).

The first step to experiencing salvation is to admit that we are sinners and we can't save ourselves (see Luke 5:31-32). Next, we need to find a Saviour who can save us (see Acts 16:31). After that, we need to go to the Saviour and spend time with Him. This includes daily devotions, Bible study, prayer, witnessing, and sabbath-keeping. We must cooperate with Jesus, maintain our connection to Him, and have regular communion with Him.

6. *What is evidence of salvation?*

"For this is the will of God, even your sanctification ..." (1 Thessalonians 4:3 - KJV).

We are born again and sanctified through the Holy Spirit. The Holy Spirit renews our minds, writes God's law of love in our hearts, and gives us the power to live holy lives.

7. What should follow when we experience salvation?

"Now the fruit of righteousness is sown in peace by those who make peace." (James 3:18 - NKJV).

All human beings have been infected with sin—sickness—and are subject to death. Our Master Chef engages workers or cooks to help do the "prep work" of sowing seeds of truth so the lives of those around them can be saved.

THE LESSON

Sin is like a deadly disease. If it is not treated, it will kill us all. Salvation is the process of making the sinner well. It is healing of the sinner's heart and the mind. Jesus, the life-giver, is the great Physician. He can heal any illness no matter how hopeless it may seem, but you have to call on Him. You have to trust Him. He accepts walk-ins—no appointment is needed—and He still makes house calls.

THE TAKEAWAY

Today, if you realise you are sin-sick, if you are not doing well, I recommend Jesus. He is waiting to heal all who are willing to come to Him to drink from the cup of salvation. Listen to the still, small voice and do the things the Lord says so you may be saved and have eternal life.

Baby Food and Drink

"A time to kill, and a time to heal; a time to break down, and a time to build up." (Ecclesiastes 3:3 - KJV).

DID YOU KNOW?

Children with strong bones have a better chance of avoiding bone weakness later in life. Parents can help by making sure children get three key ingredients for healthy bones: calcium, vitamin D, and exercise.

1. **Calcium** is a mineral that is known for building healthy bones. It is found in dairy products, beans, some nuts and seeds, and leafy green vegetables. It is also often added to foods like orange juice or cereal.

2. **Vitamin D** helps the body absorb calcium. We get vitamin D from foods like fatty fish, mushrooms, and eggs and from exposure to sunlight.

3. **Exercise:** Activities like walking, running, jumping, and climbing are especially good for building bones. They are called weight-bearing activities because they use the force of our muscles and gravity to put pressure on our bones. The pressure makes the body build up stronger bones.[28]

I still remember the morning my brother fell out of a tree and broke his leg. I think the shock was greater than the pain. Thankfully, his leg mended quite nicely, and today, he stands straight and tall at six feet four inches.

---

[28] "3 Ways To Build Strong Bones", https://kidshealth.org/en/parents/strong-bones.html

78

Having strong bones in childhood is a good start for bone health throughout life. Timing is everything, as almost all our bone density is built as children and teens. People are mostly finished building bone around the age of twenty. As adults, we still replace old bone with new bone, but more slowly. As older adults, our bones get weaker over time.

In this study, we will discover what ingredients are key for growing in Christ.

1. *According to 1 Peter 2:2, what is one ingredient necessary for growing in Christ?*

"As newborn babes, desire the pure milk of the word, that you may grow thereby." (1 Peter 2:2 - NKJV).

A new babe who desires to grow in Christ needs to take in regular portions of the Word of God. Like dark green and leafy vegetables, taking the milk of God's Word helps build good bones.

Like greens, the Bible may be taken in a variety of ways: eaten raw (memorization), tossed in a salad (read aloud in a group setting), steamed (daily personal Bible reading), and pulverised in a smoothie (weekly Bible study). There is no limit!

2. *According to Mark 1:35, what is one ingredient necessary for growing in Christ?*

"And in the morning, rising up a great while before day, he went out, and departed into a solitary place, and there prayed." (Mark 1:35 - KJV).

Anyone who intends to develop a strong relationship with Christ must spend quality time in prayer, bathing in the sunshine of God's presence. Being in the presence of the Light of the World (see John 8:12) will provide the necessary nourishment for a victorious Christian life (see Colossians 4:2).

In the manner that vitamin D builds the immune system and provides resistance to brittle bones, a habit of daily prayer makes the new believer more resistant to temptation (see Matthew 6:13 and Matthew 26:41).

3. *According to Colossians 4:5-6, what is one ingredient necessary for growing in Christ?*

"Walk in wisdom toward them that are without, redeeming the time. Let your speech be alway with grace, seasoned with salt, that ye may know how ye ought to answer every man." (Colossians 4:5-6 - KJV).

I remember a tee shirt my friend Naresha wore at university. It was the colour mustard and was emblazoned with the words: *"Walk with Jesus, exercise your faith"* and had a pattern of little footprints. Walking is a good weight-bearing exercise.

Walking in wisdom and redeeming the time includes sharing your faith with those who are not in the faith. A new believer grows in faith by being a witness to others. Being a witness is a wise use of time. Colossians 4:6 advises that when sharing his or her faith, one's speech must be seasoned with salt. In other words, what is said should be tasty and tactful.

4. *According to Psalm 27:4, what is one ingredient necessary for growing in Christ?*

"One thing have I desired of the LORD, that will I seek after; that I may dwell in the house of the LORD all the days of my life, to

behold the beauty of the LORD, and to enquire in his temple."
(Psalm 27:4 - KJV).

When the new believer spends time in the house of the Lord (see Psalm 84:4), praying and praising God, basking in the light of the Sun and Shield (see Psalm 84:11), he or she receives instructions for living a life of obedience (see Psalm 119:105) and receives answers to his or her prayers. This results in a life of rich blessings (see Psalm 84:12).

5. *According to Hebrews 10:24-25, what is one ingredient necessary for growing in Christ?*

"And let us consider one another to provoke unto love and to good works: Not forsaking the assembling of ourselves together, as the manner of some is; but exhorting one another: and so much the more, as ye see the day approaching." (Hebrews 10:24-25 - KJV).

The bones in the body are of various shapes and sizes and have different functions. The three tiny bones in the inner ear (ossicles) play a vital role in helping to maintain balance. The 33 individual bones in the spinal column (vertebrae) impact posture, our ability to walk, and help to hold our heads upright. Our ribs help protect vital internal organs such as the lungs and heart. The majority of human beings are born with 12 pairs.

Fellowship with a body of believers is critical for healthy growth in new believers. Those who are stronger and older in the faith can provide support and foster the development of spiritual babes. Teaching, training, and mentoring are key components to encourage a culture of discipleship.

THE LESSON

Ecclesiastes 3:3 speaks of *"a time to kill and a time to heal; a time to break down and a time to build up." (KJV)*.

Study of the Scriptures, obedience to the Word of God, prayer, witnessing, practicing good time management, meeting regularly to worship God, and fellowship with like-minded believers are essential disciplines for new and not-so-new believers. When one or more of these components are missing, the believer is weakened, and the body of believers is prone to fractures and breaks.

THE TAKEAWAY

We must be alert to the lures of Satan that threaten to draw us away from the faith and the body of Christ. We must kill bad habits in our lives, things that destroy our spirituality and weaken our resolve to follow Christ. Finally, we must build healthy habits—such as those outlined above—into the skeletons of our lives. That is the only way that the Spirit of God can put life into our bones (see Ezekiel 37:4-6).

REJOICE...

"… *It is* good and fitting *for one* to eat and drink …" (Ecclesiastes 5:18 - NKJV).

Royal Icing

"A time to cast away stones, and a time to gather stones together; a time to embrace, and a time to refrain from embracing." (Ecclesiastes 3:5 - KJV).

DID YOU KNOW?

- Royal icing is a pure white icing that dries to a smooth, hard, matte finish. It is a mixture of powdered icing sugar, egg whites, and water. Besides its lovely finish, it also colours beautifully, which adds to its versatility of use. Royal icing is not only for coating cakes but can also be used for intricate piping and decorations such as flowers, borders, and lettering.

- Legend has it that Queen Victoria and Prince Albert's multi-tiered wedding cake, with its nine feet circumference, was the first wedding cake to be decorated using white icing. It is said that this icing was subsequently named 'royal icing' in honour of this royal marriage in 1840.[29]

My mother's father was a carpenter with an eye for beauty and a love for hard work. We believe that the recipe for him living to celebrate his one-hundredth birthday was hard work, plus the grace of God and the exercise he got on his many trips while riding his bicycle to visit people.

I was blessed to grow up in a house he helped build. The original fence in front of the house was made of orange clay brick. It was a landmark in my village and served as a "bus stop" for people who

---

[29] "What's What About Icing"
https://cakeschool.co.uk/whats-what-about-icing/#:

travelled by bus. Grandad also loved church and spent many hours working on beautifying his church's premises. This study looks at the church.

1. *What is the church?*

"There is one body, and one Spirit, even as ye are called in one hope of your calling." (Ephesians 4:4 - KJV).

The invisible church is a community of believers who confess Jesus Christ as Lord and Saviour. A popular metaphor for the church is "the body of Christ" (see Romans 12:5).

2. *Who established the church?*

"And he is the head of the body, the church …" (Colossians 1:18 - KJV).

Using the analogy of stones, the church community is built up from living stones (see 1 Peter 2:5) who are grounded in Jesus, the Chief Cornerstone (see 1 Peter 2:6).

3. *What is the primary purpose of the church as expressed in 1 Peter 2:5?*

"Ye also, as lively stones, are built up a spiritual house, an holy priesthood, to offer up spiritual sacrifices, acceptable to God by Jesus Christ." (1 Peter 2:5 - KJV).

*   *Spiritual houses*

In 1 Peter 2:5, the church—the body of believers—is compared to living stones, part of a spiritual house. The individual believer becomes a living temple, a spiritual house or dwelling place for God to dwell in (see Romans 12:1 and 1 Corinthians 3:16).

- *A holy priesthood*

While an earthly priest would offer physical sacrifices in the earthly temple services, one purpose of the spiritual body of Christ is to offer spiritual sacrifices (see Romans 12:2). These sacrifices include an individual's will, praise, and thanksgiving (see Hebrews 10:5-7 and Hebrews 13:15).

4. *What is the primary purpose of the church as expressed in 1 Peter 2:9?*

"But ye are a chosen generation, a royal priesthood, an holy nation, a peculiar people; that ye should shew forth the praises of him who hath called you out of darkness into his marvellous light." (1 Peter 2:9 - KJV).

One of the privileges of the believer is to be an ambassador of the royal kingdom of righteousness, to show off God's glory—His character—while living in a world of darkness.

5. *How do the members of the church stay connected to each other?*

"And let us consider one another in order to stir up love and good works, not forsaking the assembling of ourselves together, as is the manner of some, but exhorting one another, and so much the more as you see the Day approaching." (Hebrews 10:24-25 - NKJV).

Fellowship with like-minded believers is vital for the survival of the community of believers. Coming together regularly to pray and study the Word, to encourage each other in the Lord, and to serve others will be even more important as we get nearer to the day of the Lord's coming.

"For here we have no continuing city, but we seek the one to come." (Hebrews 13:14 - NKJV).

> 6. How can believers of the body of Christ make an impact for the kingdom of righteousness while living in the world?

"Show respect for everyone. Love Christians everywhere. Fear God and honor the government." (1 Peter 2:17 - TLB).

One of the best ways that believers can make a difference in this world is to practice loving those around them who are different. When we practice love and do what is best for others, it will open doors of opportunity for us to walk through to speak words of truth, life, and healing and to serve them.

THE LESSON

In Ecclesiastes 3:5, Solomon speaks of two curious pairs: a time of casting stones and a time for removing them, and a time for embracing and a time for refraining from embracing.

By the throwing of stones, an agricultural field is marred (see 2 Kings 3:19), or, as expressed in 2 Kings 3:25, is destroyed, and by gathering the stones together and removing them, it is brought under cultivation.

THE TAKEAWAY

The enemy of souls will throw lying stones into the fields of believers' lives in an attempt to destroy the faith community. Those of the household of faith must apply the truth of God's Word to retrieve and remove these lies from their hearts so that they can be healed. Then can we embrace the truth as it is in Jesus—the Truth—see John 14:6, and rebuild our lives upon the foundation stone of the Rock of Ages. What a beautiful day that will be when we no longer embrace Satan's lies!

A Piece of Cake

"In the morning sow thy seed, and in the evening withhold not thine hand: for thou knowest not whether shall prosper, either this or that, or whether they both shall be alike good." *(Ecclesiastes 11:6 - KJV).*

DID YOU KNOW?

- The tradition of saving the top layer of a wedding cake dates back to the nineteenth century when it was saved as a symbol of good luck. The tradition gained traction in the Victorian era, as many couples adopted this custom as part of their wedding reception celebrations.

- The tradition states that the couple should save the top layer of the cake as a way of remembering their special day and the commitments they made to each other. The cake was tucked away and served to celebrate the couple's first anniversary.

- Some couples would also save the top layer of their wedding cake for the celebration of the birth of their first child.[30]

My husband and I saved a piece of one of our wedding cakes in our refrigerator and ate it weeks after our wedding. It didn't last for a whole year though! Thankfully, *that* sweet tradition was not the key to our marriage surviving for all these years!

---

[30] "Why Do Newlyweds Save The Top Layer of Their Wedding Cake?", "https://www.blackstockestate.co.uk/blog/weddings/why-do-newlyweds-save-the-top-layer-of-their-wedding-cake/#:~:text=

GOD'S ELECT

In biblical language, the remaining piece of cake would be called the remnant. This concept is found in many places in the Bible, with the word appearing 91 times in the King James version of the Bible. It often meant that which was left or saved from a larger portion of something; for example, in Joshua 23:12-13, Joshua was warned about the danger of God's chosen people intermarrying with the remnant from enemy nations—those left after God had defeated them on His people's behalf.

Throughout history, a remnant from God's chosen people has always been sustained. When it seems the truth is about to be destroyed, it miraculously remains, carried on by God's elect. Let's discover what pertinent messages God has for His elect.

1. What are the distinguishing features of the remnant described in Revelation 12:17?

"And the dragon was wroth with the woman, and went to make war with the remnant of her seed, which keep the commandments of God, and have the testimony of Jesus Christ." (Revelation 12:17 - KJV).

The remnant has the following distinguishing features:

- Are the seed of or descendants of the woman (the church) (see Jeremiah 6:2).
- Keep the commandments of God.
- Have the testimony of Jesus Christ.

The remnant represents the Christians of the last generation, living just prior to the second advent of Jesus. The dragon makes war on them for keeping the commandments of God, including the sabbath, and for having the testimony of Jesus Christ.[31]

2. When will the remnant become prominent?

"And the woman fled into the wilderness, where she hath a place prepared of God, that they should feed her there a thousand two hundred and threescore [1260] days." (Revelation 12:6 - KJV).

Since the remnant people are the descendants of the woman, it is important to understand the point in time when the 1260 days of Revelation 12:6 occurred. Using the day-for-a-year principle of interpretation of Bible prophecy (see Numbers 14:34 and Ezekiel 4:6), historicists conclude that this time period is symbolic of 1260 literal years aligned with significant events in church history. The 1260 years are said to have begun in 538 AD and ended in 1798 AD.[32] The remnant will play a vital role in world events in the last days of earth's history.

3. What does it mean to keep the commandments of God?

"For this is the covenant that I will make with the house of Israel after those days, says the LORD: I will put My laws in their mind and write them on their hearts; and I will be their God, and they shall be My people." (Hebrews 8:10 - NKJV).

Keeping the commandments means living by its principles of love, living in loving obedience to God (see John 14:15), and showing love to humanity (see John 13:35). The remnant of God will find

---

[31] Ellen G. White, Spiritual Gifts Volume III, page 26.2

[32] "The Day-For-A-Year Principle", March 30, 2024
https://preprod.aws.amazingdiscoveries.org/read/articles/the-day-for-a-year-principle

great joy in upholding the principles of righteousness embedded in the law of God and will hide it in their hearts (see Psalm 40:8, Revelation 22:14).

4. *What is the "testimony of Jesus"?*

"I fell down at his feet to worship him, but he said to me, "Don't do it! I am a servant together with you and with other believers, all those who hold to the truth that Jesus revealed. Worship God!" For the truth that Jesus revealed is what inspires the prophets." (Revelation 19:10 - GNT).

According to Revelation 19:10, the testimony of Jesus is "the spirit of prophecy." (KJV). This is rendered in the GNT as "the truth that Jesus revealed." Jesus came to testify/give evidence/reveal the truth about His Father's name/character (see John 17:4, 6). The remnant of God will testify of the true character of the Father (see John 14:9).

5. *What is the mission of the remnant?*

"And he said unto them, Go ye into all the world, and preach the gospel to every creature." (Mark 16:15 - KJV).

In revealing the truth about God's character, the remnant also has the awesome responsibility of preaching a special end-time message commonly known as the "three angels' messages." Each angel brings a specific message, with the second and third angels' message building on the previous angel's message. The key to accurately understanding the entire message is to understand each of the three messages.

6. What is the message of the first angel?

"Then I saw another angel flying in midair, and he had the eternal gospel to proclaim to those who live on the earth—to every nation, tribe, language and people. He said in a loud voice, "Fear God and give him glory, because the hour of his judgment has come. Worship him who made the heavens, the earth, the sea and the springs of water.""" (Revelation 14:6-7 – NIV).

The first angel's message links the eternal or everlasting gospel message—the good news—with worshipping God as the Creator.

7. What is the message of the second angel?

"A second angel followed and said, 'Fallen! Fallen is Babylon the Great, which made all the nations drink the maddening wine of her adulteries.'" (Revelation 14:8 – NIV).

In this context, Babylon is a symbolic representation of the kingdom of Satan and represents religions that misrepresent the character of God. The second angel's message is, don't trust religions that intoxicate the world with incorrect views of God.

8. What is the message of the third angel?

"A third angel followed them and said in a loud voice: "If anyone worships the beast and its image and receives its mark on their forehead or on their hand, they, too, will drink the wine of God's fury, which has been poured full strength into the cup of his wrath. They will be tormented with burning sulfur in the presence of the holy angels and of the Lamb. And the smoke of their torment will rise for ever and ever. There will be no rest day or night for those who worship the beast and its image, or for anyone who receives the mark of its name." This calls for patient

endurance on the part of the people of God who keep his
commands and remain faithful to Jesus." (Revelation 14:9-12 -
NIV).

The third angel's message builds on the first and second angels'
messages. The message is that those who choose Satan's beastly
methods of coercion and not be healed of sin will experience the
full effect of what sin does when God lets people reap the fruit of
their choice to reject the truth about God's character (see Romans
1:24, 26, 28).

THE LESSON

It is a special privilege to be a part of God's elect—a group of
people who, like Elijah the prophet, will speak for God in the last
days. The mission is simple: to preach the gospel in the context of
the second coming of Jesus (see Revelation 14:13-14).

THE TAKEAWAY

According to Ecclesiastes 11:6, it is not for us to decide what shall
do well and what shall fail. We are to do the work of proclaiming
the everlasting gospel to those who need to hear the message and
leave the work of conversion to the Holy Spirit.

Dream Wedding Cake

"Two are better than one; because they have a good reward for their labour. For if they fall, the one will lift up his fellow: but woe to him that is alone when he falleth; for he hath not another to help him up." (Ecclesiastes 4:9-10 - KJV).

DID YOU KNOW?

- Royal icing will stay firm for a long period of time, which is why royal icing is the most popular choice for destination weddings or for long periods of travel.

- Fondant icing is a traditional wedding favourite made from powdered sugar, corn syrup, and water, which is melted together to form a thick paste that gives the cake a very smooth and polished appearance.

- Most people are confused by fondant icing because of its contrasting chewy texture and sugary taste. Fondant is very easy to peel off a cake, and it is common for wedding guests to remove the fondant icing, choosing to just enjoy the cake instead!

- Ganache icing is made by mixing chocolate and cream together, making it possibly one of the most delicious icing options available.

- Because royal icing is similar in taste and texture to fondant icing, ganache icing is sometimes layered underneath them both for a delicious flavour.[33]

---

[33] "How To Choose The Best Icing For Your Wedding Cake", https://sweetbitescakes.co.nz/choose-best-icing-wedding-cake/

I was on a recent international trip from Kingston, Jamaica, to Barbados via a connection through Miami International Airport with five colleagues from work. Due to unforeseen air traffic congestion, the aircraft from Miami to Kingston was almost two hours late. Consequently, the flight from Jamaica to Miami was late. Our estimated arrival time in Miami coincided with the boarding time for the connecting flight to Barbados.

Since the international travel rules required us to collect our bags in Miami, clear immigration and customs, then do the necessary security checks, all before boarding the plane to Barbados, it was too narrow a window for us to make the connecting flight.

Thankfully, everyone got onto the first flight to Barbados early the next morning. The best thing about missing our flight was seeing members of our small team working together throughout the experience.

This study will take a look at unity in the church.

1. *What is unity?*

"There is one body, and one Spirit, even as ye are called in one hope of your calling; One Lord, one faith, one baptism, one God and Father of all, who is above all, and through all, and in you all." (Ephesians 4:4-6 - KJV).

Unity is oneness. For a Christian, it encompasses being a part of the body of Christ, having the same belief system, worldview, or faith (see Ephesians 4:13). A Christian worldview revolves around the battle of good and evil—the great controversy—and our role in it.

2. What is one metaphor that depicts unity in the church?

"For as the body is one, and hath many members, and all the members of that one body, being many, are one body: so also is Christ." (1 Corinthians 12:12 - KJV).

The human body is a fitting metaphor for unity in the church. The apostle Paul used it to demonstrate the harmonious relationship that should exist among the members of the church.

3. Why is unity needed?

"For as we have many members in one body, but all the members do not have the same function, so we, being many, are one body in Christ, and individually members of one another." (Romans 12:4-5 – NKJV).

Although the members of the body of Christ are one and are dependent on one another for growth and development (see Ephesians 4:25), they are not uniform. They have different roles and different ways of thinking, speaking, and behaving. The spirit of unity is needed for the parts or members of the body to work together (see Ecclesiastes 4:9-10).

4. How will unity be manifested in the lives of believers?

"... till we all come to the unity of the faith and of the knowledge of the Son of God, to a perfect man, to the measure of the stature of the fullness of Christ." (Ephesians 4:13 - NKJV).

The unity of the faith will be seen when there is knowledge of the true character of God—of His perfect character of love, exemplified in the life of Christ. By this shall all know that we are followers of Christ, when we have love for one another (see John 13:35).

5. *What is the source of true unity?*

"Endeavouring to keep the unity of the Spirit in the bond of peace." (Ephesians 4:3 - KJV).

It is only through the presence and transformative power of God in our lives (manifested through the Holy Spirit—the third member of the Godhead) that we can live in unity and peace with each other (see Romans 12:18).

6. *What is evident when unity is missing from the body of believers?*

"Wherefore putting away lying, speak every man truth with his neighbour: for we are members one of another. Be ye angry, and sin not: let not the sun go down upon your wrath: Neither give place to the devil. Let him that stole steal no more: but rather let him labour, working with his hands the thing which is good, that he may have to give to him that needeth. Let no corrupt communication proceed out of your mouth, but that which is good to the use of edifying, that it may minister grace unto the hearers. And grieve not the holy Spirit of God, whereby ye are sealed unto the day of redemption. Let all bitterness, and wrath, and anger, and clamour, and evil speaking, be put away from you, with all malice: And be ye kind one to another, tenderhearted, forgiving one another, even as God for Christ's sake hath forgiven you." (Ephesians 4:25-32 - KJV).

A lack of unity in the body of Christ can manifest in lies, anger, stealing, evil speaking, bitterness, malice, unkindness, and lack of forgiveness. Since the Holy Spirit is necessary for unity, discord among the brethren suggests the absence of the Spirit and the need for renewal (see Ephesians 4:23-24), revival, and healing.

7.   *What will happen when the body of Christ is united?*

"And all that believed were together, and had all things common; And sold their possessions and goods, and parted them to all men, as every man had need. And they, continuing daily with one accord in the temple, and breaking bread from house to house, did eat their meat with gladness and singleness of heart, Praising God, and having favour with all the people. And the Lord added to the church daily such as should be saved." (Acts 2:44-47 - KJV).

When people heard the preaching of the gospel and saw the genuineness of the believers of the early church, they were led to follow the God they worshipped and join the community of faith.

THE LESSON

The saying in Jamaica is, "Teamwork makes the dream work." The verses in Ecclesiastes 4:9-10 remind us that we need each other for the body of Christ to work optimally. We cannot all function as the same body part (member). Each person must use their unique gifts to make teamwork more than a dream.

God loves individuality. Like the wedding cake layered with ganache icing, every believer in the community of faith has an important role to play. The end goal is to reflect the character of God in this world—to show off His attribute of love for all of His creation—so that everyone may know that God is love (see Jeremiah 31:34 and Hebrews 8:11).

THE TAKEAWAY

We are privileged to use our diverse qualities, gifts, and talents to achieve the common goal of showing love to God, our Creator, and His created beings (see Jeremiah 31:35).

ABOUT THE AUTHOR

Colette Guthrie is a dedicated Christian who loves to study the Word of God. Her interest in Bible study was born when she attended Sunday School at the local neighbourhood church as a child. Baby steps on her journey of faith led her to attend the Inter Schools Christian Fellowship (ISCF) group on the campus of high school, where she first accepted Jesus Christ as her personal saviour.

Her search for truth led her to search the Scriptures. She became a member of the Seventh-day Adventist Church as an adult. She currently volunteers as an adult Sabbath School Teacher at the Linstead Seventh-day Adventist Church.

Colette has led several online small group Bible study sessions with church members and friends over the years. She loves to memorize Scripture and share her love for the Word of God and the God of the Word with those around her.

To connect with Colette, visit her website at https://thoughtstothewise.com and follow her on IG, FB and LinkedIn.

Email: info@thoughtstothewise.com to join her mailing list.

www.ingramcontent.com/pod-product-compliance
Lightning Source LLC
LaVergne TN
LVHW051811080426
835513LV00017B/1905